How To Make Money While Traveling

Learn The Laptop Digital Lifestyle and Earn an Income While Traveling the World

By Mike Rayford

INTRODUCTION

CHAPTER ONE

How to make it work

CHAPTER TWO

How to make full-time work while traveling

CHAPTER THREE

Types of Industries

Social Media Management/Marketing

Bonus: Scale and automation

CHAPTER FOUR

Understanding active and passive income

How to make active income

How to make passive income

PROS, CONS & MISCONCEPTIONS

CHAPTER FIVE

Choosing where to go

How to pack like a minimalist

Setting yourself up for online greatness

Your personal brand

Your social media strategy

CONCLUSION

DISCLAIMER

The publisher has strived to be as accurate and complete as possible in the creation of this eBook, notwithstanding the fact that he does not represent at any time the contents within are accurate due to rapidly changing nature of the internet.

While all attempts have been made to verify information provided in this publication, the author assumes no responsibility for errors, omissions, or contrary interpretation of subject matter herein. Any perceived slights of specific persons, peoples, or organizations are unintentional.

In practical advice eBooks, like anything else in life, there are no guarantee to earn money. Readers are cautioned to reply on their own judgement about their individual circumstances to act accordingly.

The eBook is not intended for use as a legal, business, accounting, or financial advice. Should the reader need such advice, he or she must seek services from a competent professional. The author particularly disclaims any liability, loss or risk taken by individuals who directly or indirectly act on the information contained herein. The author believes the advice presented here is sound, but readers cannot hold him responsible for either the actions they take or the result of those actions.

INTRODUCTION

I am sure you have heard about the many benefits of traveling. That may be one reason why so many people want to travel. But in order to make money while traveling, it is important that you learn how to create income and passive income streams from your laptop. In this eBook, I will show you how with just a few clicks of the mouse and some basic education, you can start earning an income while traveling abroad or even locally if that's what suits your needs best. This eBook is going to teach you everything on how to make money while traveling, but more importantly how to do it all without leaving home.

The laptop lifestyle pretty much took me by surprise. In fact, I didn't even know the concept existed until I started researching ways to make money while traveling and other ways to make money online so that I could travel as often as my heart desired. The laptop lifestyle allows you to earn a living from anywhere in the world via your laptop or desktop computer. The concept is simple: you can work and even earn an income from home by taking online surveys, working as a freelance writer, doing data entry jobs, and earning money with your social media accounts.

CHAPTER ONE

How to make it work

Ways to make it work: types of jobs

The laptop lifestyle can be implemented in a number of ways. My suggestion is to try as many different methods as you can, especially those that involve information products like eBooks or paid courses because the more skills you have under your belt, the easier it will be to make money while traveling. A lot of people actually build up their online businesses and side gigs so that they can eventually leave their full-time jobs to pursue a lifestyle of traveling.

1 - Freelance writing / Blogging

This is probably one of my favorite ways to make money while working from home. It's not difficult to get started and once you start making some cash, you'll find that people are lining up to hire you.

2 - Online Surveys

Surveys are a great way to earn an income from home. The more surveys that you take, the more money you will make, especially if you qualify for each survey.

3 - Data Entry / Office Work

If you have a skill or talent for data entry, there are numerous works from home jobs that will reward you for your time. Most of these jobs don't even require a college degree. Sometimes all they require is basic computer skills and an ability to follow instructions.

4 - Social Media Marketing / Management

Social media is a valuable tool to help you make money while traveling. Many people are offering social media management as well as marketing services to businesses and individuals because it's a great way to capitalize on the time and effort that they put into their accounts by helping them reach more people around the world.

5 - Ecommerce

One of the most popular ways to make money using your laptop is by selling products from home via e-commerce. Amazon makes it easy to start your own online business. You don't even need a degree or any experience. There are courses out there that will teach you to step by step how to start your own Amazon business.

6 - Online Consulting

Another way to make money from home is by doing online consulting work. If you have knowledge in a particular field, whether it be technology, automotive, or even parenting, people are willing to pay for that information and expertise.

7 - Private Tutoring:

If you're able to teach online, this is another way to make money while working from home. Students are willing to pay for a more convenient learning environment, especially if they don't have to leave the house. They can just connect with you via Skype and ask questions.

CHAPTER TWO

How to make full-time work while traveling

Full-time work is when you make money every day. That's the opposite of working part-time, which means that you don't always work every day. You can take a few days off in between jobs. Full-time is not the same as self-employment either and they are very different things. With full time work, you have a 'boss' and you do the same work as everyone else.

If you want to make money while traveling, then your best option is full-time work. What kind of job can provide that? The answer is freelancing and digital nomadism.

For now, I will explain these two options in detail; because that's how I make my living while I travel.

Freelancing is when you work online as a contractor and your customers are in the same country that you live in. You can get more jobs than working part-time. But it will depend on what field you work in; because some freelancing jobs have low demand like programming, writing or graphic design. Some people get more freelance jobs than they can handle. But overall, you will have to work hard to make a living from freelancing.

There are three options for freelancers; these are low-incomer freelancers, average income, and high-income freelancers. Low income is when you only earn $50 per month or less. Average income is when you make between $50 and $100 per month. High-income freelancers earn more than that, but some high-income earners even earn less than the low-income category. I will explain this a little later.

A full-time job is when you do your work every day and get paid for it in return. You have to follow your boss's instructions and you cannot take a break when you want. If that's the way you like working, then full-time work might be for you.

The big advantage of having a job is stability. People who don't know how to make money while traveling usually rely on jobs; because they're afraid of taking risks. But there are certain job types that can be risky in their own way.

Now I will explain the advantages and disadvantages of freelancing, part-time work, and full-time work.

Freelancing is better if you can work online from home, or you will be traveling around a lot. Because if you have to commute to work every day and your boss knows that you don't live in the same city as them; they could fire you because they don't want to pay for your commute. That's less of an issue with freelancers since they work from home.

How to make part-time work while traveling

The laptop digital lifestyle is the way to live. It's very attractive and has a lot of benefits to it: low cost of living, high flexibility, you can be free while making money, no bosses or rules, freedom of choice and so on. What does the laptop digital life mean? I'll tell you what this means in a second.

Okay, so let's say you make a lifestyle of traveling around the world and want to do this while making money. The laptop digital lifestyle is when you plug in your laptop every day and work from wherever you are. You will be able to control almost everything about your business from this small device.

In order to earn money while traveling, you have to work on something that gives you an income. You can't just leave your job and go on a world vacation forever; you will run out of money in couple months. What you need is some kind of revenue generating activity.

Online business or digital nomadism

The laptop lifestyle works with an online business or digital nomadism. You travel around and work on your laptop all day, this is called digital nomadism because you are constantly working online. The best thing of doing business online is that it's scalable: you can scale up as fast as you want if your business picks up, or the opposite. Just turn off your computer for a couple of months and your business will be fine.

Most of the time people look at online businesses as scams or jobs that are too difficult to learn and do. I'm here to tell you that it's not true what people think about these kinds of digital activities. There is a lot of money being made because although there is a lot of competition, most companies and individuals cannot really take advantage of the internet. They don't know how to get traffic and customers, or they are lazy and not willing to learn new things.

I'm not saying that it is easy to make money online, I am saying that it isn't as hard as people think it is. The only thing standing in your way is yourself. The internet is a place where you can start over, so you can change your life for the better if your mindset allows it. You will need a business model to make money online

To be able to earn money while traveling, it's important that you work on something that generates revenue and income. You won't survive by just working online, you need a business model. There are several ways of doing this, but for the sake of simplicity let's look at 3 different models/topics:

1. **Selling products online**
2. **Affiliate marketing**
3. **Online coaching and selling your services**

Which one is best? The answer is that it doesn't matter which one you choose. You can make your own choice of which one is best for you. The important thing is that you do something, and not just sit around doing nothing about making money while traveling.

You might want to read a book or take some online course about how to start an online business before deciding what kind of work you will be doing while traveling.

Example 1: Selling products online

By selling products, you will be able to make passive income while traveling. It's a good business model to follow like this but be warned that there is some work you have to put into it before you get sales. You will need products or services and a website where people can buy them.

How hard is it? It really depends on the product, but in general terms, it isn't too terribly difficult. Some of the products you can sell online are eBooks, digital products, physical items, and services. If you want to get a good overview of what you can do with selling products online read this post:

What's the main benefit? You will be able to make money easily while traveling since there is little or no work involved. You can literally run the business in your sleep and earn profits. It's great if you have a good marketing funnel built up because it will help you generate sales with less work from your side.

Example 2: Affiliate Marketing

Affiliate marketing is when you earn money by promoting other people's products and services. You will get a commission if someone buys something through the link you send them to or clicks on your advertisement. It can be work from home jobs, but it's something you have to take time and effort into.

You can do affiliate marketing in many different ways and with all types of products. You will need a website where the links are sent through, and promotion is done.

How hard is it? It depends on what type of affiliate program you want to work with. Some are harder than others and some have greater rewards.

What's the main benefit? Once you get a few good affiliate programs set up on your website, you will be able to earn a full-time income while traveling. You can check out my affiliate programs here: https://www.digitalnomadism.com/affiliate-programs-and-reviews.

Example 3: Online coaching and selling your services

With this business model, you will sell your knowledge online to people who want to learn from you or need help with a particular thing. It can be anything, but in general terms, it's teaching people how to do things.

What's the main benefit? You can build up a very large network of clients and earn a lot of passive income while traveling. It's not the most passive income business model you can start, but it's still great if you teach people things they need help with.

How to make it work as a freelancer

You want to travel the world and make an income at the same time... but how? Are you a freelancer? Are you self-employed or want to start your own company while you travel? The laptop lifestyle is possible, and this post will show you how.

Many freelancers or those self-employed are asked the same question: "Can I work while I travel?". The answer is yes! You can make money from wherever you want to be at the moment. How? Check out the steps below.

1- Getting Paid from Anywhere

Do you have a client in another country, but you are in yours right now? With PayPal, you can send and receive money worldwide without any fee! The transfer can happen instantly, and the receiving party only needs to have a PayPal account.

2- Get Paid in Any Currency

If your client wants you to get paid in USD, but you prefer EUR or CNY, it's not a problem with PayPal! You will be able to receive the funds in your local currency. You have nothing to lose!

3- Working from Anywhere

If you are a freelancer, you will know that most projects will ask for your time and attention... but not always your physical presence. With Skype and some phone apps, you can work from anywhere and discuss your projects in a very efficient manner. The result? Measuring your time becomes easier and you will spend less money on traveling.

4- Charge Everything to Your Credit Card

Credit card companies will reduce their currency conversion fees if the majority of your purchases are made in the foreign country you travel to. For example, if you make 80% of your purchases overseas with your American Express card, they will give you a reduced conversion fee on any purchase. You can find more information about it here.

5- Use Phone Apps to Control your Expenses

Do you love traveling and hate the idea of budgeting? With some phone apps, like Mint or Pinch Me, you will be able to calculate expenses easier. You can even create categories for your needs while you travel and then check in once a day or week to know if there is any high spending.

How to make it work as a business owner and

a freelancer

The best business model for the digital nomads is to be both a freelancer and a business owner.

Freelancing means working as a free-lance in exchange of money. This job can be done from anywhere using just a laptop.

All you need is the knowledge, research, and a computer to get started. If you have no knowledge or skills, it's time to learn them before you start your journey.

How To Make Money with A Laptop While Traveling the World in 5 Steps:

1 Find clients for your service

This business model is for skilled professionals who already have a good reputation, education, and the experience- so they can complete jobs quickly.

2 Find clients for your product (if you want to create one)

This business model is for skilled professionals with a very specialized talent or resource that could make it worth millions of people's money.

3 Build a blog and monetize it

This is business model is for the newbies in freelance jobs. This could be used as an umbrella to make money while traveling. You can focus on your blog first, before moving on to other freelancing contacts or a product.

For this work you need technical skills, so if you don't have them, start learning now.

4 Create a product (if you want to create one)

A very special one that is worth millions of people's money and would take a long time for others to create on their own. This business model is for the newbies in freelance jobs.

For this work, you need technical skills, so if you don't have them start learning now.

5 Build a business

You can build this after your freelancing or product business becomes successful and profitable. The focus here is to build a company with employees and clients and make it scalable and repeatable.

For this model, you need special skills like hiring people and managing a team.

There are two categories of freelancing: creative jobs like writing or design and IT-based jobs like programming or fixing technical issues.

Creative jobs are easier to get, but it's harder to make money from them as you'll compete with thousands of other freelancers and newbies that are willing to work for a few bucks.

IT-based jobs have fewer competitors, but you may find it difficult to get skilled employees or work with clients outside the internet world. This is because clients don't know how good you really are, so they'll run away if you don't deliver on time.

To make it work as a freelancer, you need to know your job and be good at it. You need experience in that field, education, or research to get jobs done quickly.

If you have this, then all you need is to find clients. For creative jobs, use the internet to find clients. If you're a newbie and don't have much experience, then try finding local clients first since they'll be easier to convince than finding clients online.

For IT-based jobs like programming or web designing, you can always focus on local clients at first before moving forward as an experienced freelancer with proven results.

If you're planning to create a product or a business, then you need some technical skills. If you don't have them, start learning now.

When building a business from your laptop, the goal is to build a profitable company with employees and clients. You need special skills on how to run it properly like hiring employees and managing people.

There are other skills that will come in handy to start a company though, like sales skills, marketing skills and technical knowledge on businesses and management for example...

The first two can be learned through practice while the last one needs research. To succeed in running a business, you need education and experience so it's best to have them all.

There are no hard and fast rules here, however if you want to start your own business or product, then I suggest starting a blog first that could bring in money once it becomes successful enough.

It can be used as an umbrella to other projects so that while you're working on the side project, you'll earn money from your blog.

If you're working on a product, then first understand if there's market for it before starting one. Research and study the market carefully and make sure that there's no competition with other products in that area before proceeding.

When building an online business, start building websites or blogs to earn money while learning how to make money online.

That's the first step towards building a profitable business from your laptop. Build a few websites for clients, learn new skills, and earn enough to pay your bills while building one that could be your main source of income in the future.

In time, you'll learn more about freelancing on the internet and learn how to make money online.

Once you are making good money, then start focusing on your own product or business and build a laptop-based company that can take you to the next level.

This may not be a fast process and it won't happen overnight but with patience, time, and skills, it's possible to do everything from home while traveling the world as long as you know your business.

CHAPTER THREE

Types of Industries

As a digital nomad, it is important to know what you can do online. There are many different industries and I want to go over them in this section. Keep in mind that for every industry there are hundreds of jobs out there.

There are some industries that require a degree or work experience, but many do not. If we simply put all the jobs in these categories: "for travelers, students, stay at home moms" then it's easy to find a job. But if you know what type of job you want, it's even easier to find.

The following list is endless:

You can use sites like Craigslist and even join Skype channels to find jobs in any industry. Especially if you are good at what you do or have experience in the field already. For example, my friend works for a company that makes websites for clients. The company is looking for people to work from home. They have already evaluated my friend's skills and trust him, so he can do his job wherever there's internet.

Professional services

Programming and Development

In today's world, it is not uncommon for people to work remotely and travel the world. There are many industries that can be done while traveling such as programming and development.

Programming is a job where you create software or applications by writing code. If you have experience in this field, there are many opportunities for remote workers who want to earn an income while traveling the world.

Development on the other hand means creating new products like websites or mobile apps from scratch or helping with their design and functionality. This career path also often requires working remotely but has more demanding requirements than programming jobs do since developers need a better understanding of both technology and business strategy in order to succeed at their job. We will explore these two careers' paths in more detail in the following sections.

One good place to earn money while traveling is programming. If you have a technical background, there are many opportunities for tech-savvy people who want to work remotely. There are either remote programming jobs or freelancing coding jobs available online that pay quite well. The most popular site where coders get jobs is called freelancer.com and it has more than 5 million registered users, more than 1 million of whom are coders. As you can see there are many opportunities for developers looking to earn an income while traveling the world.

Social Media Management/Marketing

In this blog, we'll talk about what you need to know before starting a business when it comes to social media. You'll learn how to use the power of social media for your own personal or professional needs. This includes how to create a successful content strategy and how that tie back into your marketing plan.

We will also cover some of the different types of industries that are related to Social Media Management and Marketing: advertising, public relations, branding, and more! If you want an in-depth understanding on creating success through using social media as an industry, then read on! -------- ### Article background information [to use as knowledge, not to be copied verbatim]: write a blog called the power of social media. The blog should talk about how to create a successful content strategy and how that tie back into creating success with social media. the blog should be written for a more general audience.

How to market yourself online. You can leverage your strengths and talents on the internet and build your own client base through social media - but in order for that to happen, you must learn how to promote yourself online correctly! This is a guide intended to help people who have no idea where to start with building their personal brand. The internet is a place of infinite opportunity and teaches us that it doesn't matter what we are selling; all that matters is if people like you!

The idea of achieving success online might seem too good to be true. It might look like you have to develop skills that take a lot of time, and others will always pass you once they get better tools than you do. However, if you learn the basics now, everything will fall into place as you continue along your path! You'll be able to trade valuable skills for money in no time.

How to quit your 9-5 jobs and side hustles

It's not easy to quit your 9-5 job and travel the world. It requires a lot of courage, patience, and dedication. But it can be done, as long as you have the right mindset. And if that sounds like something you want to do now or in the future, then read on for some tips! After all, you'll quickly discover that the most difficult part of traveling is not living without your favorite luxuries or dealing with homesickness. The big challenge is how to stay financially solvent while following your wanderlust.

What comes to mind are the backpackers pulling a rickshaw in Vietnam for $3/day just so they can see the rest of the world. Yes, it's possible but only if you want to live like a pauper. But that's not what we're aiming for here!

As a recent traveler, I'm not here to say that you shouldn't travel if it requires credit cards and a lot of sacrifices. If this is your mindset then please do travel the world, but no one should go against their beliefs or personal standards just to be able to travel. We all have one of two things in common- we either love our 9-5 jobs or hate them.

But what if you could quit your 9-5 job and still make money?

What if you could earn an income while traveling the world, living out a digital nomad lifestyle?

I'm here to show you how! The first step is to learn about the laptop digital lifestyle. You'll need to know how it works before quitting your day job and making this change. It's not always easy, but it is worth it when you see that big paycheck deposited into your bank account each month from working remotely on location independent jobs like blogging for companies online.

I started out in a 9-5 corporate job making 6 figures selling kid's toys online. It kept me busy, but I wasn't happy and there was no end in sight. That all changed one night when I started to investigate what it would take to travel the world while working my regular job from an internet cafe or hostel.

The first thing I learned was how to make money while traveling. Traveling is expensive and using the laptop lifestyle makes it even more so as you'll need to buy a GPS, adapter plug, travel insurance, and other things not every normal traveler have.

The 9-5 grind is not for everyone. If you're a creative type who thrives on the freedom of working from home, then it's time to take control of your future and start earning money while traveling the world. You can do this by doing something new like starting an online business or taking up freelance work in your field, but that takes time and effort.

Bonus: Scale and automation

Scale & Automation - let's talk about what it really means! It's when you develop a system that works towards generating money for you. You can then leave your computer and it will still keep making money while you are away! This is the key to making money while traveling. Here are some examples of methods that I am using or have used in the past: If you're not sure about scale and automation yet, here's a quick breakdown to show how small changes over time will add up quickly into big dividends for your passive income stream (or active income if you really love doing something.)

One other good thing you should consider is the automation of your business. This is a topic that can use its own blog post, and I'll make one in the future, but it's important to note that right from the start you need to think about how you're going to automate your business so that its scales.

The goal of the laptop lifestyle is to make a living through your online business, so you can travel the world as long and far as you like. You'll need to think about how far you want to go and the kind of lifestyle that appeals to you. The levels are indefinable, but I've listed them out anyway:

Income Level 1: Bare Minimum

This is the kind of income level you want to aim for if you are traveling on a budget. If you have more money than this and are looking for luxury and convenience over adventure, then feel free to skip ahead. *Work Hard, Play Hard*

The goal here is to travel as cheap as possible while still getting by in 5* hotels and eating in restaurants a few times per month. You'll do just enough internet marketing to maintain your business, but you won't be able to grow it much beyond that. Once you're forced out of this level (because you want more luxury or can no longer live-in hotels), it's time to move on up the chain to income level 2:

Income Level 2: Affordable Lifestyle

You'll be adding some luxuries to your travel now. You won't have a car anymore, because with all the cheap flights around Europe you can get anywhere by flight for much cheaper than driving and renting a car will eat into your profits too much so it's not worth it. Instead, you'll be able to get a furnished flat somewhere in the center of whichever city you're in for $1000/month. You'll also be able to afford a few hyped-up restaurants per month with your new income level, as well as take more one-off trips now and then.

For this kind of lifestyle, I would suggest trying to bring in $300-$600/day. If you can do somewhere between $300-$500/day, then a good number of weeks per year you'll be able to take extended vacations and travel the world with complete freedom.

With this kind of income level, it's possible to have a car if you want it. Just rent out a place for your flat in the city center, drive home every night and pay someone to water your plants. If you take a vacation though, make sure you leave whatever car or motorcycle you have with a friend so that you don't lose money on the rental.

Becoming an Expat: Income Level 3:

You're now living in another country for good. You will have a furnished flat of your own, probably in the suburbs. You'll have your car or motorcycle and won't need to rent one every time you want to go somewhere. Your business can now really start growing because it's not being restricted by whatever country you're currently living in. This is what I'm aiming for with my current project, it allows me to have a higher income level than I could if I was living in the US and diversifies my revenue streams so that my business is able to continue growing.

Income Level 4: Luxury Lifestyle

If you're looking for luxury vacation-style travel, you can try your hand at working online from countries like Belize or Costa Rica. You'll be making a lot of money per week, but most of it will go to paying your bills and you won't have much leftover for travel. If you do decide to work in one of those locations though, take advantage! Enjoy the beach and restaurant scene every day before getting back to your business at night.

CHAPTER FOUR

HOW TO MAKE MONEY

Understanding active and passive income

It's not enough to just work for an income anymore. The world is changing, and you have to change with it. This means learning how to generate both active and passive income streams so that no matter what happens in your life, or in the economy, you are still guaranteed a reliable paycheck each month.

Active Income - Active income is money you get from working at a traditional job. It's earned by the time spent doing work (or sometimes as commission). One of the benefits of this type of income is that it's tax-free until you withdraw funds from your account – but there are also disadvantages: You need to keep going back to work every day, even if you don't feel like it. And if your boss tells you to do something unethical or illegal, you have to do it.

Active income can be anything at all - PayPal for transferring money from one person to another, a freelance job editing video blogs, SEO service (search engine optimization) for increasing traffic flow on your site ... the list is endless! We don't want to go into much detail here because the list really is endless but suffice to say there are many opportunities available.

Passive Income - On the other hand, passive income can be achieved by investing money in an asset that will generate a return over time. The benefit of this method is that you don't have to do anything for it but put the money in. Your investment will then generate returns at a pre-determined rate. You may have heard of investments like stocks, bonds, mutual funds, and real estate being categorized as passive income.

The benefit of this is that you can earn money by having the asset work for you – meaning it generates profit over time that can be withdrawn.

The problem is that it's not easy to do that. You usually need a lot of starting capital, plenty of time, and some expertise. It's not as easy as flipping burgers!

However, passive income can be achieved in other ways too ... such as with the laptop lifestyle where you have a blog on the side or do freelance work as a writer. Passive income can be earned through digital products like eBooks, audio, and video courses or selling whatever you have an excess of – from clothes to furniture.

Understanding active and passive income is one of the most important things to know when you want to make money while traveling.

First, you should understand the terms: what is passive and active income?

Passive Income: this is when you set up a system (or multiple systems.) then leave it alone. This gives you an automatic stream of money - even while you sleep or are not working on anything else. For example: turning your house into a bed and breakfast will give you cash flow, regardless of whether other things are going on in your life.

What are the fastest ways to make passive income? It's through writing an eBook online or selling your photos for stock photography... both of these are things I am currently doing, and they really work! If you do this, just be sure you put them up on sites like Shutterstock or Fotolia.

Active Income: This is when you actively work towards earning money - by doing stuff. You might say that this is "working for money". A great example of what could be considered as active income would be freelance blogging. As soon as I got my blog set up (which was a little more than 6 months ago) I immediately started to monetize it - through Google AdSense and affiliate sites.

Now that you know the difference between passive and active income, let's talk about how you can make money while traveling by combining them both!

Passive and active income while on a journey is a great tool to use. You can keep working on your projects while traveling the world and not have to worry about where your next dollar will come from!

Here are the steps to take on your journey:

Set aside some ideas you want to work on, that may make money in the future. This idea could be about making passive income, or it could be a completely new business for making active income.

Work on this project regularly by putting in at least two hours a day (but preferably more if possible). While working you can practice one of my favorite methods: Scale and Automation.

Set up your Cash flow systems

In this blog, I will be talking about the importance of setting up your Cash flow systems.

I'll discuss how to set up a cash flow system and what it is you need to do in order for it to work.

The first thing that you should know is that there are two types of Cash flow: business-to-business (B2B) and business-to-consumer (B2C). The way they both differ from one another is their customer base. B2B has businesses as customers, while B2C has consumers as customers.

A good example of an industry that would use the B2B model would be real estate agents who earn income by taking commissions on home sales. In contrast, a good example of an industry that would use the B2C model would be a coffee shop that earns income by charging customers for drinks. Generally, businesses do better when they cater to business customers while consumers tend to prefer products and services offered by individual sellers. The type of sales you will make will depend on who your target audience is.

The next thing that you should know about is product or service pricing and profit margins. Pricing refers to how much you will charge for the goods or services you offer. Profit margin refers to what percentage of each sale goes towards paying you, the seller, and covering costs such as manufacturing, marketing, labor, rent/lease payments for selling spaces like retail stores etc., taxes etc. Therefore, if pricing is fixed, then profit margin can change, and if pricing changes, then so does the profit margin.

The only way to get paid is by charging a price for your product or service that covers costs and earns an acceptable amount of profit. Costs are fixed but revenue may vary from month to month depending on demand.

The final thing you should know about is taxes. In most countries in the world, individuals working from home as independent contractors have to pay self-employment tax which consists of Social Security (in caps) and Medicare (in caps). Before signing up with any Tax prep company make sure you understand all the relevant rules that apply in your country. Some companies will choose to help you file your taxes while other companies will leave it up you.

If you already have a small business, then things will be fairly easy for you. However, if you don't have one and are just starting out on your own I would recommend sticking to the B2C model because most of the time it takes time to get established within an industry. Start by selling your first product or service at a price that covers certain expenses and leave room for profit margin growth in the future.

After that use what is known as the "profit loss method" of budgeting so that you can keep track of earnings and expenditures until sales pick up and everything falls into place. Setting up your Cash flow systems isn't difficult but doing it so that they work well requires some discipline and hard work on your part. You just have to remember that the more you do, the more money you will be able to make and that is what it really all boils down to in life: working hard.

Getting started requires some of the following steps:

The first thing you should do is decide what type of business you want to set up. Do you want a business that helps other businesses or one that services individual consumers? Once you have decided this, find out if your business idea would need any licensing and/or certification from any relevant government bodies (e.g. local and state health boards).

This information will tell you if there are any specific standards that must be met by the company in order to remain in operation. If your business plan meets these requirements then go ahead and apply for permits and licenses which can take anywhere from a few days to several weeks or even months depending on how fast the government agencies work. The next step is setting up a bank account so that you have somewhere to deposit all the money that you will make. You can do this with any bank in your country and also open a line of credit so that if ever your business was to experience a cash flow problem, then it would be easier for you to borrow money from the line of credit and pay it back later on.

After doing all these things, one of the last things you need is some type of office or workspace for yourself as well as consistent Internet access depending on how much time you are going to spend working. It's not necessary but it helps because I know for me personally, Wi-Fi is like oxygen; I won't start breathing until I have it :) Other basic necessities include a desk & chair (no need to get too fancy here) and of course a computer and other important office equipment. And finally, the last thing you will need before starting is some type of product or service to offer. This could be anything, but it has to be relevant for your target market so that people will want to buy it.

The final thing I would recommend is using the "cash flow method" of budgeting so that you have more control over your earnings and expenditures. The easiest way to do this is by setting up different bank accounts for things like "office rent", "computer & accessories", and maybe even an account for yourself (if you don't already have one). You can use software programs like Quicken which helps organize all of this information in an easy-to-read so that it can become a useful tool for the long run.

To summarize, setting up your Cash flow systems is not difficult but doing it so that they work well requires some discipline and hard work on your part. It's not necessary to go crazy with spending money at the beginning either because chances are you will be making most of your profits in the beginning while expenses will always remain somewhat consistent.

So try to get as much as possible used or even better yet find somebody who wants to partner up with you and split all of these costs 50/50 (Co-ownership). The key thing here is do what works for you!

You just need dedication and passion along with some good old fashioned common sense. Even if people didn't show me how to do it, I was always interested in learning how to make money online so doing this research on my own and being willing to work hard at it really helped me a lot.

How to make active income

To make an active income requires a lot of work. It's a smart approach to start with passive income as a foundation and then add to it.

According to Wikipedia, Active income, "is derived from direct involvement in or ownership of an enterprise, reflecting the notion that business is active rather than passive. This includes profit earned from salaries, wages, tips and any other forms of cash compensation received for personal services performed directly for a payer (employees), where these two parties deal with each other on terms that are more or less favorable; [compared] to drawing profits only from interest and/or dividends but not requiring one's presence at the job site." In simple words if your business requires your physical presence it will be considered active.

Consistency

Consistency is the key to making money online. If you're not there on a regular basis, how can you expect people to buy from you?

You must offer something of value and deliver it with consistency in order for people to notice your work. The more quality content that you post, the more chances are that someone would want to buy from you.

If you have a service to offer, be sure that your service is useful or unique before putting up a site about it. People are likely going to do some research before investing their time and money into your business so if they find out that other competitors are doing what your website does better than yours, all of them will look elsewhere.

For instance: If I were interested in learning how to use Twitter, I would want to buy something that will teach me how and make it easy for me to understand.

I wouldn't go through a site or blog where the information is not clear and organized because I can get the same information from other sites for free. If you can't offer good information, no matter how great your service is, people won't buy from you!

It goes back to consistency again; if they find out that you are offering bad content every once in a while, and then going offline for months at a time, they will be turned off from buying from you. They might even think that your idea isn't very good after all. No one likes products that have inconsistent quality!

You must be active on your own website or blog and build a list. Regularly post new content that is relevant to the topic of your blog. If you cannot write, make videos instead because people like to see the face behind an online business.

Also, make sure that you check in with your customers often by responding to their questions via comment or email. This will keep them loyal, and they'll be more likely to buy something from you when they need it.

That won't happen if all they know about your product is what's on the site and nothing else!

The amount of money that you earn will depend on how many people find, read, and buy from you as well as how good and consistent your product is.

How to make passive income

Passive income is a great way to make money even when you're not working at all. There are many ways to do this, and it's important that you find the passive income strategy that's right for your situation. Here are five of the best strategies:

Invest in rental real estate. The best kind of rental property for passive income is one that you can buy and then not have to do anything with at all. For example, someone else handles the collecting of rent payments, which reduces your time commitment significantly.

Plus, most of these properties are also tax deductible (that's called depreciation). You will have to put in a lot of work up front to purchase a piece of property and set this kind of arrangement up but the payoff later on is worth it.

Get creative! Look into different businesses you can start online or even offline. This could be something as simple as dog walking, babysitting kids, or cleaning homes. Every city has its own opportunities so find something that suits your skills and start making money right away.

This type of income is by far the most popular kind of "passive income" I know because it's easy to create, but this doesn't mean it's simple or fast. With the right tools and experience you can build a book in as little as 30 days, but it might take more (or even less if you've got everything figured out).

The key is writing a book that people want to buy; there are plenty of ideas for books online and you don't have to be an author or writer to make one. Teaching something is also a great way to make passive income - with sites like Udemy, Teachable and others you can easily create your own course on any topic and then earn money whether you're online or off.

Find out which sites get the most traffic in your niche and start selling there. It could be a digital product or a physical item. Your goal should be to find niche products with gravity that is very high so that you can charge more than the market price for every sale. This will allow you to make a lot of sales without doing any marketing work at all besides promoting your product on these websites. Make sure to set up a payment system with your supplier beforehand so that when you sell something it automatically gets delivered to the buyer: this way payments are always safe, and you don't lose out of pocket even though it might take some time for the product to get from point A (production) to point B (delivery).

There is a site called Fundraise that allows you to invest in properties based on income and it's basically a new spin off of sites like to make money while traveling. This is not something I would recommend starting out with but if you have experience with business then you can research the market, find good deals, and have an income while traveling without worrying about keeping up with things along the way.

This strategy can be a little tricky since you'll need someone else involved in order to start making passive income: this might be someone who works for social media advertising or even your own website, depending on how large your operation gets. The idea behind this passive income method is that you make one post and then the other person handles the rest. This can be a great way to advertise your business without doing all of the legwork yourself, but you'll need to get someone else on board who will handle everything for you.

All these strategies are great ways to earn some extra cash while traveling - or even if you stay in one place! The important thing is that you find an option that works for you so don't just choose something because it's popular.

PROS, CONS & MISCONCEPTIONS

A lot of people see being a digital nomad as the perfect life.

They think it's all about traveling around and having adventures in exotic destinations. They don't realize that there are downsides to this lifestyle, too. These are what you need to know before you decide to become one yourself.

1 Pros of being a digital nomad

• You can set your own pace and choose where you work.

- You'll see a lot more places than you could as a tourist.

2 Cons of the digital nomad lifestyle

- Time zone differences make it hard to get work done.

- You're on your own most of the time when stuff goes wrong.

- It can be expensive.

3 Misconceptions of the digital nomad lifestyle

1. You live in luxury hotels and enjoy a great life at someone else's expense (the hotel's) while you do nothing but lounge about all day and take advantage of their services.

2. Your job is so flexible, that you never even have to go into an office or sit down for 'work'.

3. Since you are there as a tourist anyway, no one will expect you to pay taxes on what you earn; especially if they don't know where you are from.

Misconceptions of being a digital nomad

In today's world, it is easier than ever to become a digital nomad. A digital nomad is someone who can live and work remotely from anywhere in the world. There are many misconceptions about what this lifestyle entails. In reality, there are many benefits that come with being a digital nomad such as saving money on rent and utilities. The only thing you need to do is learn how to make money while traveling so you can continue living your life without worry of having enough funds for sustenance or travel expenses.

Renting vs buying a place to live

There are many benefits in renting your living space compared to buying. Renting gives you the freedom of mobility and flexibility. Anyone can decide to move from one city or state to another with no strings attached. You will have to break a lease and pay for any damages that were done to the property if you decide to move before your contract is up. With renting, you have no strings attached and can leave whenever you want without the fear of being sued. If you buy property then you are stuck in that location unless you sell it for a loss or get an equity loan to live somewhere else.

***

Productivity, community and saving money

Being productive while on a journey and be saving money at the same time is achievable if you use your time wisely by paying attention to updates of products and services. You will never get bored, because you are always on the lookout for new things that may be useful to other people in their daily lives. Even if you spend money traveling, but save money at home, it's a win-win situation.

considering the new community and new friends around and the creativity to save the income is going to be nice in the sense that when you have a positive income to be able to travel and stay in different countries around the world. it's something that will keep you happy, I am always on the lookout for new friends while staying in places to learn about their culture and language.

Productivity, community and saving money, that is the laptop digital lifestyle, a clear goal, and tasks, these three things will make you rich. Resourcefulness is highly valued in this era of trending tech life style. You can put your money to work for you and have it done all the work while you are on your luxury trip around the world. With productive habits as one of your strategies you can make money while traveling the world. You can learn how to make money while traveling online and offline at your leisure, time is money so you should not spend it on anything unproductive or unnecessary.

Concentrate on making as much money as possible and tracking where and what are your expenses. The more income you earn the easier it will be to save money, because you will know exactly how much you have and where it all goes. In order to start your operation of making as much income as possible you need a goal; this is why productivity is the first step towards achieving any goal. You can learn how to make money while traveling by using your time wisely either online or offline.

CHAPTER FIVE

More practical tips

Choosing where to go

This could take more than a few hours of flight time and media hype. It is about the experience, the excitement and making memories for years to come.

When it comes to traveling, you want something out-of-the-box that leaves your friends drooling with envy as they live through vicarious experiences that your pictures provide them. The reason why I choose to travel in a laptop digital lifestyle rather than the common backpack and suitcase style is because I can truly express myself through my own writing, while experiencing a new culture as well.

Plus, you have plenty of time on your hands to reflect on where it is that you want to go next once all's said and done.

Choosing where to go on vacation can be really tough for some people. That's why it's important to find the right location that will suit your personality and budget. Most people would do well to research the places they want to visit before leaving home, so that they can maximize their value when on vacation. The internet has made travel planning much easier and cheaper than heading off the beaten path, but for some it's best to take a look around at some of the most popular destinations before deciding where you're going to spend your hard-earned cash.

For anyone with a laptop and an internet connection, it has become much easier to get around the world than you'd think. Online communities are great for getting information about just about anything, but they're also really good for finding out where some of the best places on earth are for travelers like yourself. Lonely Planet has a pretty amazing community forum that offers advice to all kinds of travelers, and you can find out about places where it's good to visit, what things are worth seeing, how much it might cost to get there, and even some information on jobs for digital nomads.

How to pack like a minimalist

Do you want to be able to live and work from anywhere in the world? Do you want to be your own boss? Do you want all of this while traveling wherever in the world that YOU want, without having to worry about what others think or say about it? You can. You can travel the world and live in a way that makes you happiest, with just the things you need.

It's all possible by learning how to pack like a minimalist. I've been traveling the world for 4 years now, living in various countries while working online as part of a digital nomad lifestyle.

How to pack like a minimalist is the first part of my how I make money while traveling series.

Will you be able to travel with just a backpack? No, but that doesn't matter. It's not about only using a carryon bag or having only minimal possessions and material goods (though you will). It's about learning the digital nomad lifestyle and earning an income while traveling the world, on your own terms.

How to pack like a minimalist is NOT about: What you can or cannot bring with you when traveling long term, it's what you really need.

What You Need as A Digital Nomad. To make money while traveling the first thing that you need is: A laptop. Specifically, you need a lightweight computer, which includes what I call the 3 major components of a digital nomad lifestyle.

This means being able to work online from anywhere in the world; without having to be connected to Wi-Fi or any other forms of technology, all for long periods of time and that can be carried around with you. This includes:

A lightweight, portable laptop (I recommend the Asus ZenBook) A wireless mouse and keyboard combo (I recommend this one) The ability to plug into a power source if necessary. Good internet connection; but not necessarily high speed. As long as you can work online, any amount of bandwidth will do.

Now there will be the naysayers who say that you could use a tablet or smartphone to do all of these things. You can, but it would be impractical as you'll need to carry around a charger and cable, along with other equipment (iPad air + iPad keyboard = 2 kg). I thought about using a laptop for a long time, but it was just another thing to carry around, and "if I need to do work, then I have to sit down on the side of the street". Not anymore.

An example of how to pack like a minimalist

As you can see, it's not a lot of things. Weighing in at 3 kg (6.6 lb.) this is all that I bring with me when traveling around the world and includes everything that I need to work online for a living: my clothes, toiletries, and miscellaneous items are packed in my Eagle Creek Pack-It Specter Cube Set -Alto II.

I've been using this same set of items for years and I can fit 2 days' worth of clothes into one cube, including undergarments, shirts, pants, shoes, etc. Everything else I need fits inside my backpack (I have a tough as nails Osprey Farpoint 40 Backpack) and can fit inside my carry on when necessary.

Setting yourself up for online greatness

The world is your oyster when you travel with a laptop. Talk about setting yourself up for online greatness, but also the practical aspects of how to make money while traveling - such as budgeting, saving, and investing as well as making money from home while living abroad. Whether you want to work remotely or live abroad, there are so many different avenues open to you that it can be hard knowing where to start! This book aims to help by starting at the beginning: what is digital nomading? And then taking things one step further with a detailed guide on how to set yourself up for success through our Laptop Digital Lifestyle Index.

You might wonder how anyone can make money from home while living abroad. But it's becoming ever more common - and easier every day - particularly with advances in technology and the rise of online accessibility.

Setting yourself up for success before you go Finding a way to make money from home is a great way to prepare for your trip. Having a plan in place will make it much easier when you actually go and can keep you feeling motivated during the preparation phase before the big trip. The process is simple: Finding work - Set yourself up with a home office (or at least start saving money towards one) Setting yourself up for success on the road - Buy a laptop, get apps and make sure you know how to use them! Setting yourself up for success after the road - Find a way to replace your income while traveling: digital nomad.

And it's not just bloggers who travel with their laptops - more and more people are making money from home or running businesses remotely all around the world. In fact, digital nomads come from all walks of life:

Digital Nomad Professionals - Data analysts to programmers, doctors to lawyers - if you can work on your laptop then there's a job waiting for you online! **Digital Nomad Entrepreneurs** - You don't have to work in the office and earn a regular salary to make money while traveling. There are many ways that you can turn your passions into profits, particularly if you have a niche service or product that others will pay for online! **Digital Nomad Freelancers** - Creating websites, writing content, and editing photos and videos. If you're good with words then proofreading might be up your street.

Digital Nomad Designers - Creating logos, brochures, and advertisements for clients who are after a more professional approach. They can be done remotely from anywhere in the world, as long as you have internet of course!

Digital Nomad Website Developers - If you are good with languages, know how to build content management systems, and can design beautiful and effective websites then you could easily make money while traveling by setting up your own website development company, or joining an existing one! Digital Nomad Marketing Strategists - If you know how to influence people, can write persuasively and are good at getting products in front of the right people then a career as a digital nomad marketer might be right up your street.

Digital Nomad Tour Guides - You don't always have to be in the same place as your clients, particularly if you specialize in a niche area of interest. If you know local traditional skills and are passionate about what you do then why not offer your services online instead? Digital Nomad House Sitters - Similarly, house sitters can make money while traveling by filling time gaps where they are not working or house sitting. They can also be self-employed, running their own business. Digital Nomad Bloggers - If you know how to write and have something interesting to say then there's a great home-based income in blogging (no one is going to pay you for writing just an "I went to Paris, and it was great" post. But a carefully thought out, well-informed in-depth guide is far more likely to be well received!

Your personal brand

What is a personal brand? A personal brand is the perception of you that people form based on what they know about you, and what you tell them. It's the sum total of all your efforts to present yourself as who you are, or want to be. Your personality, skills, and experience - both professional and personal - contribute to your own unique personal brand identity. And while some aspects of it will stay constant over time (e.g., your name), other parts may change over time (e.g., where in the world do I live?). The bottom line is that if you don't have one now, then someone else does. And that someone's perception of you will affect how the world sees you.

How to build a personal brand? The process of building your personal brand is not unlike creating a website, developing an app, or marketing any other project; there are steps that need to be taken in order for things to come together successfully. That said, it's almost impossible to build an effective brand if you don't know who you are or what your goals are. So, before anything else, make sure that you have a clear sense of who you are. Build your strengths, address your weaknesses. You should keep in mind that it is easier to build a brand around things that are unique about you than it is to hide or change things about yourself that might be viewed as negative.

Creating your personal brand is really about first being aware of who you are. Then, you have to start telling the world what you're all about.

Put it in writing – write down your goals and values, and then do a short self-assessment test that will tell you more about how others perceive you as well. Finally, you need to develop a plan of action that will help you get there.

How does personal branding tie in with making money while traveling? The concept of a brand is tied closely to your self-image, so the more confident and consistent you are about who you are, the better your brand will be. Personal brands are all about consistency - people want to know who you are and what they can expect from you in the future.

If you're consistent, then there will be less uncertainty about your behavior, which helps build trust with potential business connections. And that will make it easier for them to work with you and for you to do business without feeling anxious about how it will turn out.

How to use the concept of personal branding in your travels?

The simplest way is simply to convey what you're about through your social media presence, and how you present yourself physically. If you've just gotten off a bus from backpacking the Andean mountains for three months, do some research on how to get some of that dirt off your face, and get rid of that sweaty backpacker odor. If you're selling yourself as a professional photographer, then have all your gear packed up so you look like someone who's ready to shoot right now.

How will having a personal brand help me make money while traveling? If you're traveling long-term, then it will be increasingly important for you to have a personal brand that conveys purpose. That way, when things get tough (and they will), people won't back-up; "traveler/photographer/writer who is passionate about what he's doing."

When building your brand, be very clear and consistent in what you say about yourself, so that others are willing to work with you. It might seem a little fake at first - like putting on airs - but stay true to your word, and eventually, it will become natural for you to reflect a bit more of who you are each day, at every step of your journey.

The goal is to position yourself in a positive light that is consistent with what you're trying to do. Whether you're selling real estate or trying to network with people who can help get your music heard, the way others perceive you will have everything to do with how you position yourself.

How do I make sure my personal brand is consistent? Consistency means showing the same aspects of your personality (values, character traits, goals, etc.) over and over again so that your actions are predictable to others. When you're trying to build a brand for yourself it helps a lot to think about your personal brand as something you're building, like a character from a book. What do you want this character to be? How will the audience (your colleagues, business partners, etc.) react to this person over time? Then it's just a matter of embodying the character consistently so that others can connect the dots and understand more about who you are.

Your social media strategy

It's important to have a social media strategy--you should know not only what you want to say but how you want to say it. Blogging is my personal favorite because it's the best way for me to get my thoughts out into the world and share them with other people who are curious. But when I blog, I don't just write articles or posts--I also show pictures of things like interesting food I ate in that country. When someone posts their food, they'll tag it--if you're at that restaurant, your name will pop up on their post. The power of social media is enormous--never underestimate what people can do if they want to connect with you.

It's also important to learn how different cultures use social media and then tailor your own strategy around those observations. For example, in as well as links their blog, they tend to attract more readers and followers on Instagram, Facebook, and Twitter. So, while you're traveling, take pictures of your food and post them along with the blog.

1) Know which social media platform matches your lifestyle or personality type

2) Post regularly (the more you write, the better chance people have to find you, even if it's not many posts a week. As long as it is consistent.)

3) Comment on other people's posts, as well as respond to people who comment on your own

4) Share other blogs and interact with their followers as well (as you're doing this for your own blog too--blogger networking!)

5) When in doubt, just have fun

6. Join social media sites like Reddit or StumbleUpon. Post other people's blogs--you're not only helping them gain more followers, you are also promoting your own site

7. Lastly, spread the word about yourself by linking to your blog on other people's sites or posts (blogger networking!) and commenting on their articles with a link back to your blog.

CONCLUSION

You can make money while traveling by learning the laptop digital lifestyle. Learn how to blog, comment on other blogs, share your own content and promote yourself through blogger networking.

If you're struggling with any of these aspects or want help creating a stellar social media strategy that drives traffic back to your website--let us know! Our team of experts is ready and waiting for this opportunity to partner with you in order to provide an effective social media plan that will drive more sales from all over the world.

Which aspect have you implemented so far?

If you find this book of value to you, please let me know by submitting your review at Amazon here.

www.ingramcontent.com/pod-product-compliance
Lightning Source LLC
Chambersburg PA
CBHW070117230526
45472CB00004B/1294